Moles

Lori Dittmer

CREATIVE EDUCATION • CREATIVE PAPERBACKS

Published by Creative Education and Creative Paperbacks
P.O. Box 227, Mankato, Minnesota 56002
Creative Education and Creative Paperbacks are imprints of
The Creative Company
www.thecreativecompany.us

Design by Ellen Huber; production by Dana Cheit
Art direction by Rita Marshall
Printed in the United States of America

Photographs by Dreamstime (Isselee), Flickr
(gordonramsaysubmissions), iStockphoto (GlobalP, Hailshadow,
hsvrs, Ian_Redding, onlyyouqj, Ornitolog82, phototake, Santia2,
scorton, tchara), Shutterstock (Close Encounters Photo, Miroslav
Hlavko, Eric Isselee, KOO, Madlen, Petr Salinger)

Library of Congress Cataloging-in-Publication Data
Names: Dittmer, Lori, author.
Title: Moles / Lori Dittmer.
Series: Seedlings: Backyard Animals.
Includes bibliographical references and index.
Summary: A kindergarten-level introduction to moles,
covering their growth process, behaviors, the backyard
habitats they call home, and such defining features as their
long claws.
Identifiers: LCCN 2017051390 / ISBN 978-1-60818-973-1
(hardcover) / ISBN 978-1-62832-600-0 (pbk) / ISBN 978-1-64000-074-2 (eBook)

Subjects: LCSH: Moles (Animals)—Juvenile literature.
Classification: LCC QL737.S76 D58 2018 / DDC 599.33/5—dc23

CCSS: RI.K.1, 2, 3, 4, 5, 6, 7; RI.1.1, 2, 3, 4, 5, 6, 7; RF.K.1, 3; RF.1.1

First Edition HC 9 8 7 6 5 4 3 2 1
First Edition PBK 9 8 7 6 5 4 3 2 1

33614081421124

TABLE OF CONTENTS

Hello, moles!

Moles are small mammals.

They live underground.

It is always dark there.

Moles have furry bodies.
Their legs are short.

Paws with long claws
help moles dig.

Most moles
are brown,
gray, or
black.

Their tiny eyes cannot see well.

Moles find their way by smell and touch.

Hungry
moles eat
a lot.

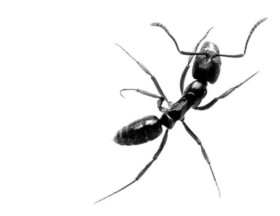

They gobble earthworms,
snails, and insects.

Mole mothers have babies once a year.

Baby moles are called pups.

They leave their mother after one to two months.

Moles tunnel through dirt.

They follow their noses
to find food.

Goodbye, moles!

19

Picture a Mole

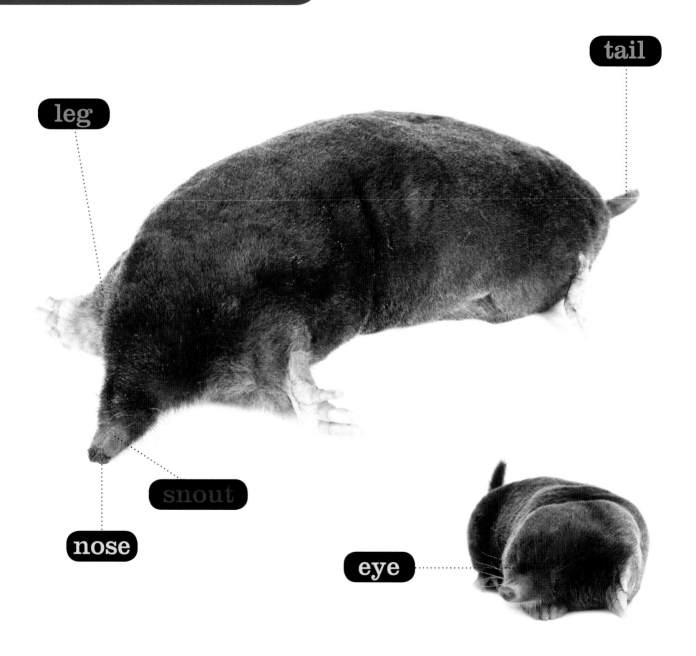

tail

leg

snout

nose

eye

fur

claw

whiskers

21

insects: animals that have three body parts and six legs but no bones

mammals: warm-blooded animals that have hair and feed milk to their babies

tunnel: to make a hole through something

Read More

Perkins, Wendy. *Star-Nosed Moles.*
North Mankato, Minn.: Amicus, 2018.

Sebastian, Emily. *Moles.*
New York: Rosen, 2012.

Websites

Activity Village: Moles
https://www.activityvillage.co.uk/moles
Print out a picture to color, or make a mole puppet.

Easy Science for Kids: Moles—The Hole and Tunnel Makers
http://easyscienceforkids.com/all-about-moles/
Read about moles, and watch a video about the star-nosed mole.

Index